by Ellen Lawrence

Consultants:

Suzy Gazlay, MA
Recipient, Presidential Award for Excellence in Science Teaching

Kimberly Brenneman, PhD
National Institute for Early Education Research, Rutgers University,
New Brunswick, New Jersey

BEARPORT
PUBLISHING

New York, New York

Credits

Cover, © Vaclav Volrab/Shutterstock, and © James Laurie/Shutterstock; 4, © Four Oaks/Shutterstock; 5, © Four Oaks/Shutterstock; 6T, © Robyn Mackenzie/Shutterstock; 6B, © Sergieiev/Shutterstock; 7L, © Four Oaks/Shutterstock; 7R, © Peter Betts/Shutterstock; 8, © senk/Shutterstock; 8–9, © Andrey Yurlov/Shutterstock; 10BL, © Maxim Godkin/Shutterstock; 10R, © oriontrail/Shutterstock; 11, © AlexanderZam/Shutterstock; 12L, © Swapan/Shutterstock; 12R, © Kenneth Libbrecht/Science Photo Library; 13, © wongwean/Shutterstock; 14–15, © EpicStockMedia/Shutterstock; 16, © Four Oaks/Shutterstock; 17, © Shutterstock; 19, © Shutterstock; 20, © Steve Wilson/Shutterstock; 21, © Linda Bucklin/Shutterstock; 22L, © Marynchenko Oleksandr; 22R, © Vaaka/Shutterstock; 23TL, © Alexander Zam/Shutterstock; 23TR, © Shutterstock; 23BL, © Shutterstock; 23BR, © Four Oaks/Shutterstock.

Publisher: Kenn Goin
Editorial Director: Adam Siegel
Creative Director: Spencer Brinker
Design: Alix Wood
Editor: Mark J. Sachner
Photo Researcher: Ruby Tuesday Books Ltd

Library of Congress Cataloging-in-Publication Data

Lawrence, Ellen, 1967-
  What is the water cycle? / by Ellen Lawrence.
      p. cm. — (Weather wise)
  Includes bibliographical references and index.
  ISBN-13: 978-1-61772-402-2 (library binding)
  ISBN-10: 1-61772-402-5 (library binding)
  1. Hydrologic cycle—Juvenile literature. I. Title.
  GB848.L39 2012
  551.48—dc23

                    2011045761

For more information, write to Bearport Publishing Company, Inc., 45 West 21st Street, Suite 3B, New York, New York 10010. Printed in the United States of America in North Mankato, Minnesota.

10 9 8 7 6 5 4 3 2 1

Contents

An Amazing Journey

It's a hot day at the zoo.

To cool off, a large elephant uses its trunk to suck up water from a pool.

Then the animal sprays water all over its body.

Some of the water falls to the ground and makes a big puddle.

The water won't be there for long, though.

The water is about to go on an amazing journey.

trunk

What do you think will happen to the water in the puddle?

Water is a liquid. It can flow and take the shape of whatever it is in. That shape might be a bottle, a pond, or even an elephant's trunk!

Disappearing Water?

As the sun shines, the puddle at the zoo gets smaller.

Soon, all the water is gone—or is it?

You can't see the water anymore, but it is still around!

The sun's warmth has changed it into a **gas** called **water vapor**.

Once the water turns into vapor, it floats from the puddle into the air.

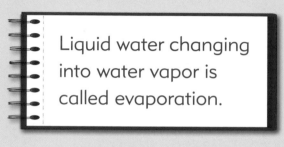

Liquid water changing into water vapor is called evaporation.

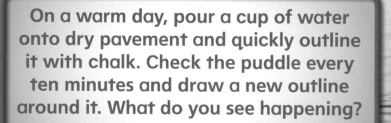

On a warm day, pour a cup of water onto dry pavement and quickly outline it with chalk. Check the puddle every ten minutes and draw a new outline around it. What do you see happening?

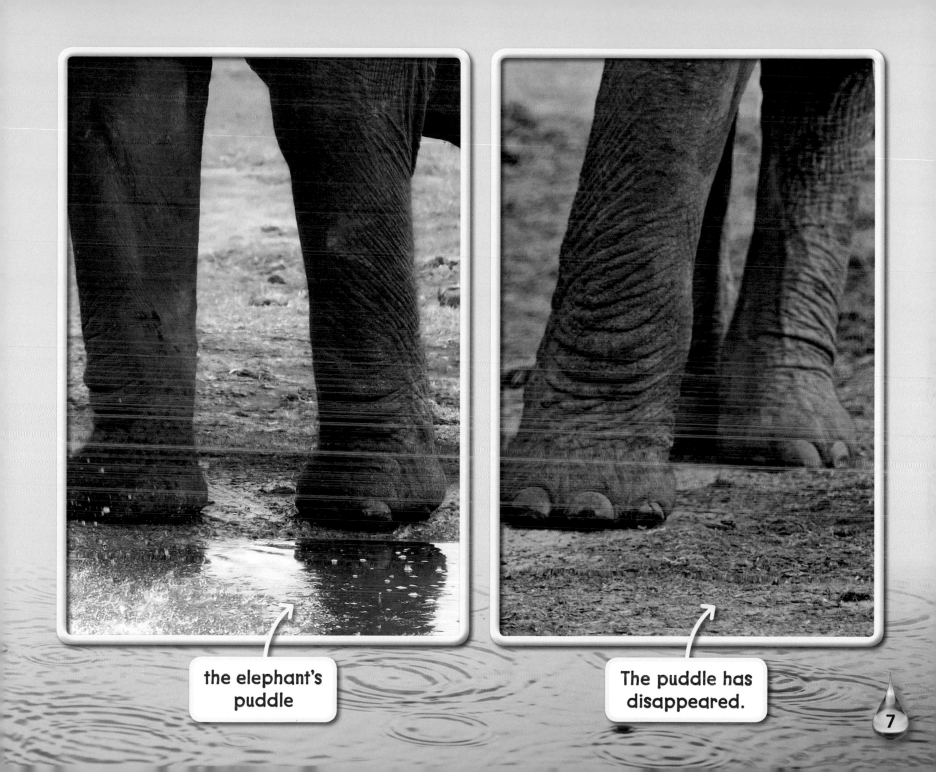

the elephant's
puddle

The puddle has
disappeared.

7

Up, Up, and Away

Soon the water vapor from the elephant's puddle has floated thousands of feet above Earth.

Up and up it rises—one mile (1.6 km), then two miles (3.2 km).

It even passes a jumbo jet!

High in the sky, the air is colder than on Earth.

As a result, the vapor gets cooler as it rises higher and higher.

When the vapor cools down, it changes back into tiny water droplets.

Water vapor changing into liquid water is called condensation.

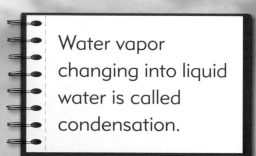

What do you think might happen to the water droplets now?

Making a Cloud

High in the sky, the tiny water droplets gather together around bits of dust.

They spread throughout the air and join up with other droplets.

When billions of water droplets join together in this way, they make a **cloud**.

The water that the elephant sprayed from its trunk is now drifting miles above Earth as part of some white clouds.

a close-up view of water droplets

Clouds may be just one mile (1.6 km) above Earth, or as high up as eight miles (12.9 km).

clouds

Making Raindrops

Inside the clouds, the tiny water droplets stick together to form raindrops.

It can take a million tiny droplets to make just one raindrop!

The wind blows the clouds across the sky.

Now the water from the elephant's puddle is spread out high above Earth and many miles from the zoo.

If the air around a cloud is very cold, the water droplets freeze. They become tiny bits of ice that stick together and make snowflakes.

These close-up pictures show a raindrop on a leaf and a snowflake. In what ways are they alike? In what ways are they different?

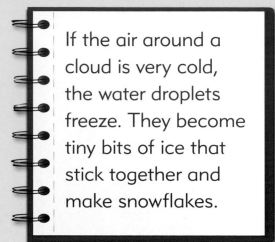

raindrop

snowflake

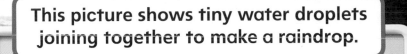

This picture shows tiny water droplets joining together to make a raindrop.

tiny droplets

a raindrop forming

Back Down to Earth

More droplets join the cloud, and each raindrop gets bigger and heavier.

Soon the raindrops get too heavy to float in the air—and they fall back down to Earth.

The raindrops splash down into the ocean.

Just a few days ago, some water drops were inside an elephant's trunk.

Now they are part of an ocean wave!

Nearly three-quarters of Earth is covered by the ocean. As a result, a large amount of the rain and snow that fall onto Earth lands in the ocean.

From a Puddle to the Ocean

Some of the water that the elephant sprayed has moved from a puddle to a cloud to the ocean.

This movement of water is called the **water cycle**.

Now that the water is back on Earth, it may someday go through the water cycle all over again.

The water that landed in the ocean might go through the water cycle again within a few days or it might stay in the ocean for hundreds or even thousands of years!